Flotsam

poems by
Catherine Kyle

More books available from:

Etched Press
San Francisco, CA
www.etchedpress.com

Also available in Amazon Kindle Store

First edition
Cover photograph by Catherine Kyle
Interior layout by Kevin Dublin
Honeynote font by Denise Bentulan (http://douxiegirl.com)

To the Pacific Northwest and everyone who loves it

Acknowledgments

Grateful acknowledgments are offered to the following publications in which these pieces first appeared, some in previous forms:

The Broken City "Spindle"
Cirque: A Literary Journal for Alaska and the Pacific Northwest "A Shipwreck off the Coast Leaves Only One Survivor"
Handful of Dust "Girldolls"
Line Zero "Casualties of a Three-Day, Island-Wide Power Outage: Peaches, Anorexia, Borders"
Lingerpost "Return"
Lost Coast Review "Dialect of Skin"
Melancholy Hyperbole "Approximation"
Poetry South "In the Presence of a Gentleman, Ephemeral"
Progenitor Art and Literary Journal "Tide Pools" & "Cleaning Fish"
RiverLit "Husband as Tin Soldier"
Riveter Review "Remkiashta"
Scythe Literary Journal "Counting Colors"
Superstition Review "Pysanky" & "The Village Remembers"
WomenArts Quarterly "The Beast"

Contents

The Village Remembers

There are very few left
still alive who remember
her glide through the mist
of the pallid summer dunes,

the way her braid swayed
like a devil's pendulum,
a hungry compass needle
pointing everywhere but north.

The sun and the village
were dreaming of progress
as Leena's starfish toes
clung like lightning to the dock.

Only two sisters,
the coral and the orchard,
spied the ring that howled
from the gully of her fist.

They watched it fiercely emptied
to the belly of the green waves,
shouting like an opal star
as moonlight pierced its side.

The village can remember,
since no one else remembers,
the fortitude of buckling,
the salt on Leena's skin.

Tide Pools

So many hopes assemble in spaces
reserved for things refused—

this shell, a womb, out of which climb
robbers who quarrel to claim new skin,

this soft eruption, bright anemone,
waving its colorful kerchiefs for luck.

Citizens travel to scry for their fortunes,
picking their way over slithering stones

to the circle of blue, the opulent mirror
that informs the moon of its worth.

Her husband's face is alchemic,
hypnotic, predicted and hungered for,

rosary-light. The shape of his journey
is hobbled, contorted, the cost of hope

rising, exhaled through sand. This is
the excess torn from the pearl; this

is the price of star-knowing. He asks
about destiny, all that they sought

and she answers that fate is a choice.
Stained glass murals shatter somewhere

unforeseen by humans. The sentient mud
in the jowls of tide pools raises its head to the sky.

Pysanky

Using the black wand, the *kistka,*
my father rakes thin rigid scars
on the egg's shut face in beeswax.

The eight-daggered star on its forest
green backdrop sings like a magpie's
tantrum netted in hope. Legends say

that the demon who alights on the
unbroken line will fall captive,
imprisoned as yolk. At five years old

I arch in to observe the exorcism and
a coil from my gold scalp crackles red,
seduced by flame. The lock disintegrates

with the sharp scent of gunpowder
until my father's fingers snap it dead
beside my ear. We stare into each other.

The wax cakes. The dark line holds.
He reports that fragility begets dissolution
except when fragility begets deft explosion.

In this moment our hearts are pulsating
pysanky: beautiful, ephemeral, and
brimming with trapped demons.

The eggs, his mother's note scolds,
must not ever be bartered.

They can only be given,
crooked mouthfuls of light.

In spring the shells will float on waves,
a pathway for the drowned.

Return

Having exhausted herself with the sights of the land,
its periwinkle petals and little brown birds,
the woman who lived at the corner of 42nd street
decided, one morning, to return to the sea.

Long had we watched her watery gaze
peer out the window from behind pale curtains
that fluttered their eyelets like cubbyhole graves.

We both knew, I think, my sister and I,
that she was not long for this world.

I imagine her cupping our goldfish's bowl,
running her nails down the smooth sheen of glass.
I imagine her running, but taking her time,
bidding farewell to the silver-armed willows
and kissing the faces of new rhododendrons,
scrunched and magenta with the effort of
growth. I am sure

that she whispered words of encouragement
to the bulbous marble eye
of our family fish,
as she emptied him,
flapping
like a tangerine kite,
into the surf,
where he was lost among the foam.

The morning's headlines spoke of her
mysterious disappearance,
the way she left nothing
but a pair of blue jeans

rumpled on the shoreline
to be trampled by the crabs.

Our father embraced us with the certitude of flannel
and gently took away our neon plastic pails.
He arranged them in the garden
near the flaking scarlet steps
and filled them all with marigolds
and other earthly things.

Cleaning Fish

That was the moment synesthesia set in—
the father's clean knife slicing belly flesh wide.

The swim bladder, stomach, pyloric cecum,
bunked with red eggs in the tent of the fish.

The scent of saltwater, Pavlovian trigger,
resuscitates clusters of life in her mind,

makes her remember the sound of her father
scraping the pearled orange sacs from the skin.

In her dreams faceless children unborn in the village
clasp hands and recite as they jab her insides,

fish, fish, your eggs will not save you,
woman, your eggs will not save you from need.

Counting Colors

On the old wooden bridge stands a woman who cups
her chin and counts colors in the water below.

The gush utters rib cage crackles of logs,
bleached long and white by the fervent gaze of August.

A young couple passes with abrasive fuchsia limbs,
flailing a small dog on a ribbon-slender leash.

The dog and thwoman exchange long looks and she fantasizes,
briefly, about biting through its chain.

She steps on the ledge with pointed red heels and wonders
(if they wonder) if she will fold herself over

like a crumpled paper note
and inchworm gracefully into demise,

so open and maternal in its forty seven shades
of outstanding purple and impeccable blue.

The dog and its joggers cross and proceed.
The woman locks stares with the dark rushing line.

She recounts the colors from her new vantage point,
noting three that had hidden in the shadow of the bridge.

As the sun carves its arc in the brilliant sky,
the shadow will retreat and she will raise

herself higher on polished, straining toes,
chasing the variety of infinite hues.

Approximation

Our grandfather points out the girl at the market
who comes to buy mushrooms and stare at postcards.

She touches the sand dollar wind chimes, retracting
her hand as the dry bodies musically crash.

She strokes the sharp scales of fish lain in shaved ice,
tries to discern the words caught in their gills.

She has forgotten the art of existence,
the plunges in green froth and roilings in sand.

Each night she stalks the interminable shoreline,
never remembering quite how to want.

The waves that once served as a million lovers
bite at her ankles and soil her skirt.

She settles for gathering fragments of white shell
and boiling them back in her kitchen with song.

She lays them in rows, where they darken the tablecloth,
places them onto her slow tongue and chews.

She is taking communion, eating a proxy,
hoping its likeness will cancel the void.

None of these things are the ocean itself.
But she has forgotten its taste.

Casualties of a Three-Day, Island-Wide Power Outage: Peaches, Anorexia, Borders

December rolls over the island
and we are shredded. Talons of wind seize
trees like fistfuls of hair and buckle full power lines,
cutting pine needle gashes in the wet and shining streets—
thin matchsticks of foliage weeping from the womb
of an emerald, detonated sky.

Abandoning the spirals of breath that rise in the air of our
      house,
we pick our way, mittens kissing, over cragged, rueful branches
that grasp our woolen ankles like fairy tale claws.
We tiptoe like doe in an unfamiliar wasteland,
seeking out breakfast and visions of moss. Eyefuls of yards
made feral by storms tense thrilling veins and cajole laughing
      spines.
In the distance, the sea churns its bottomless stomach toppling
      fish,
while the hip of the sun shifts carelessly under oyster-and-pearl
      colored sheets.

At the market, a girl in braids and a green apron
shimmers with rain and pleasant manners,
bestowing bags of frozen fruit—why keep what won't sell?
The gluey orange syrup stains her hands already, mixing with
      frost
from the cold cut corpses of slowly melting peaches.

You announce the menu—*Bloody Mary soup!*—and demand
the freshest tomatoes. Wrists wrestle paper cornucopias
of red and ready circles and thick and heavy vines
as we wander fallen branches with wiser, knowing feet.

We cook on a camp stove by candlelight and wash
our hair in enormous pots of warm and silver water,
prowling the floorboards like mermaids wearing large, ill-fitting
    shirts.
Coral fingers tussle tresses and stir the steaming brew.
The garnet liquid bubbles, purring of oregano
and I am startled to find, for the first time in years,

the feeling of hunger unabated by shame—
the ascetic corset abruptly unlatched.

At night you are all silhouette, and my curved
thoughts sway in the U beneath your ribs.
Quietly we sleep, borderless and outside of time.
Beyond the windows the sea rages on,
grey and indiscernible from sky.

Girldolls

Once we were dolls,
cloth and floppy, hands eloping,
but they told us, *hey! girldolls*
don't hold hands that way.

Can you remember? Our hairs
were strands of chaos, chattering,
conversing in the language of cracked
bells. Our scars were paused on open,
rosebud mouths that bit on secrets,
and our glass bead eyes cavorted
and our blouses were all—

> but then we changed our minds;
> remember? They told us to
> look elsewhere; they told us to
> drop hands.

The sky was so bright that day, blindingly
bright. There was, you said, no place to go—
there should have been a corner or at least
a slender shadow into which we could
have wriggled like a pair of living vines—
but the sky was so bright that day, blindingly
bright, that even the dark alleys in our
neurons waved their flags.

We cooked there on the pavement,
stranded seastars for the white gulls.
The starkness of the playground was enough
to startle God.

Remkiashta

Now and then the world haunts our eardrums with its
silence, so as she grew taller she invented needed words.

Renisive. Adjective. Resentfully resigned.
Therystic. Adjective. Awed by unearned praise.

Remkiashta. Noun. A platonic kind of lover. The thing she
decided she wanted in place of the boy who thumbed her jeans.

He told her on a bridge once how he longed to be her lover.
She stared at daisies he held in his hands and the way they all

snagged on the wind. Their voices fluttered downward,
     apocalyptic
arrows that brushed the backs of car roofs, reluctant in the rain.

She told him if he wanted he could be her *remkiashta*. Their
     knowledge
and their yearnings swerved, wet wheels across gold lines.

In the Presence of a Gentleman, Ephemeral

In the spring, cherry blossoms open,
ripe hands cupped to the sun,
and you, my visitor, arrive
in the dappling footfall
of light on the platform,
a black fedora,
the scent of old paper,
and a curious penchant for pawpaw.

On the train ride to the old capital,
a city swollen with shadow and memory,
the bones of our knees clatter a dialogue,
bruising each other with every track's turn
like heavy purple stones.

For days we subsist on tangerines—
the shovels of our thumbs discolored
by the constant plumbing of their skins—
and bean cakes so small,
golden brown beneath the plastic,
they notch in the divot of your palm.

Crows spatter the graveyard.
Rain and your ChapStick shine on my cheek
and I fear the old gardener will see.

The blossoms shut their hands
and quick as proverbial cats
walking rooftops far too thin,
we tumble out of love,
howling as we fall.

On the pavement our tails

flash down steep and crooked alleys
and under darkened dumpsters
and away.

The Beast

The beast drifts ashore,
a fallen constellation.

By morning men have gathered,
wringing dusty hats.

Who will carry off
the largest piece of heaven?

Whose wife will love him
most wickedly tonight?

The men shift their heels,
lick the salt from their whiskers.

None of them wants to be
the first one to flinch.

Nearby a sand piper steals
from its mate

and the beast begins
to reek.

A Shipwreck off the Coast
Leaves Only One Survivor

The sailor awakens to find her
unmangled, the figurehead clutched

with her wooden breasts hard.
His breath at her throat like a son

or a lover devours the scent
that rebuffed martyrdom.

He drags her, reluctant, over the gold sand,
aching a trench in its belly. The curve

is a map that traces reunion
between the shore and tide.

He does not believe in separate things.
He does not believe in reunion.

All night he traces the grain in her cheek
with a dagger gone cold from no kills.

All the men, the women, devoured by ocean,
and he, the first one to leap.

He hangs his head in the noose of his hands.
He hangs white shells from her neckline.

All he wanted to say was that
he died a noble husk.

Though both will float in comparable chaos,
the line between flotsam and jetsam is want.

One is abandoned;
the other, destroyed.

Humans distinguish the things waves do not—
he slashes at reeds for a shelter.

Mother, destroyer, salvation, eternal—
he slashes her face with a knife.

Spindle

She skips white stones
across moan-pealing
water, feeding found
coins to the wheel of
 fate, the *rota fortunae*
that swallows bright
tribute down its red
gullet, a birth in
reverse. Wood becomes
metal, metal to ash, the
cycle of progress
jammed in lockstep.
North Star, precipice,
prelude incarnate, skip
all your stones down
the foxhole of prayer.
Tomorrow the pebbles
you toss to the wheel
will all have resurfaced,
elaborate myth.

Certain Spells

She knows certain spells
        that could make a man blind.

She knows other spells
        that could make him the sea.

It is difficult to tell the difference,
        sometimes.

Fluttering, indigo—her hair
        a bright fistful of ribbons,

she unfolds the limbs
        of her compass rose heart,

its chambers and ventricles, major aorta,
        subclavian artery

beating red maps. As her promise,
        inaudible, marks his lips

violet, his hands become stingrays
        that clutch her shining voice.

Their mouths become gateways that swallow
        the stars.

She prays as he peels her
        thorns from her vines:

Claw of chance and eye of valor,
        let him be a voyage.

Gut of road and heart of lances,
        let him be a scar.

It is pointless to try to tell the difference,
        most times.

Dialect of Skin

There is no substitution
for the dialect of skin;

its absence sings of razors hurled fast at mirrored gates.

The presence of the body
and its lurid implications

intersect, square junctions on a tiled kitchen floor.

What ponderance is given
by the round, pulsating cells?

What provisions granted
by the way they all perspire?

She knows that she touches
her spine in the night,

a lean beheaded arrow, just to know
the world is there, that she gleans

secret comfort from railcars'
jostle because it means dancing

with strangers' hard knees.
She knows that the world is always

imperfect, that touch must be fed on
and famine fed on too. In giving

her body to rivers and oceans,
she tries to chase solitude out of her pores.

The water responds in the way it knows how,
by welding her hairs to each other.

Husband as Tin Soldier

Soldered together in the furnace of our marriage bed
        I the ballerina
        you the metal man

Our toes intermingle, gelatinous silver
        your rifle evaporates
        my pirouette decays

Closing our eyelids, we fly up the flue
        beauty and armament
        valor and peace

We cling to each other and cling to the fire
        becoming, surrendering
        melting to new

When all that is left is a heart made of iron
        cool it, won't you?
        place it near your skin

We Have Become the Forest

Take my hand.

        Lead me.

Through pitch and viridian.
Straight to the ocean
where the stones hulk gray.

        Take this blade.

Lead me.

        Nevermind the darkness.
        Cut your braid and leave it

        where the deer will crush its curve.

Remember that clean
was not the aim of this,

        so I will feed you honey
        and you can feed me gin.

Unclothe your scars. I would trace them with my teeth.

        Unclothe the bird that beats like fire in your
                chest.

Its small red wing is all we need, shard of heart
glimmering darkly as flint.

        Strike it against the stone of my tongue.
        Strike it again for good measure.

The fire that nuzzles
each tree like a harlot
erases the threat of return.

> The crackling trunks relinquish our initials,
> sighing great gusts of black, screaming crows.

We have become
the forest itself
and it will remember our names.

Additional Acknowledgments

Thank you, also, to Diane, Ari, and Hannah for their invaluable feedback on these poems; Zach, for so many things that happened on seashores; Jenny, for canoeing and for always inspiring me to be a better writer; Wendy, for encouraging me in writing and in most everything else; Jason, for not letting me give up; Kyle, for the many childhood talks about infinity; Lessie, for many tea dates in the winter; Will, David, Alyssa, Stefanie, Ryan, Krystal, Gwen, Jenn, Audrey, and Betsy, for believing in me, supporting me, and being generally awesome; Megan, Ashley, Elena, Laura, and Marti, for their devotion to the arts; and Kevin Dublin, for believing in this work.

Author Bio

Catherine Kyle is a Ph.D. candidate in English at Western Michigan University, where she studies representations of artists' coming-of-age stories in contemporary graphic novels. Her hybrid-genre chapbook *Feral Domesticity,* which contains poetry, fiction, and paintings, was published by Robocup Press in 2014. You can read more about Catherine on her website: www.catherinebaileykyle.com.

www.ingramcontent.com/pod-product-compliance
Lightning Source LLC
Chambersburg PA
CBHW051742040426
42447CB00008B/1258